MAKE HER SQUIRT!

LAST LONGER, BLOW HER MIND, GET HER BEGGING FOR MORE

Sarah Johansson

CONTENTS

TESTIMONIALS

All I think about now is having my man get inside me.

– Tamara Trye

He does not ask for sex anymore. I'm the one who demands it from him.

- Kerry Hammond

Introduction

The sex in your relationship has become boring. Is there a way to spice it up?

Just follow the tips mentioned throughout this book. And you can bring enjoy HOTTER, STEAMIER sex in your relationship. The book contains alot of tips on how to enjoy great sex with your partner. It is impossible to of course apply each and every tip each time you have sex. But rather, the reader should try and implement a few tips with each sex session to keep things fresh and different.

1

LADIES FIRST!

The desire for sex is like the appetite for food. The human man and woman have two mouths that need feeding. One mouth, on their head. The other mouth, down below. Both need feeding. And just like the hunger for food, the penis and vagina become hungry, too. As a man, you should focus on pleasing your woman first and fulfilling her sexual desires FIRST!

Whilst men can climax in a matter of minutes, women cannot.

Make it your primary aim to satisfy your woman first before satisfying yourself. She'll, in turn, then try harder to satisfy you.

2

GET HER FIRED UP!

If you're a man, then it's essential you understand this. YOUR WOMAN IS NOT LIKE YOU!

Men become sexually excited very easily by what they see. You could look at your woman and she could turn you on just by looking at you sexily, or walking and moving and dressing in a sexy way.

Women need foreplay! That's how they become stimulated and excited. Many women don't climax during vaginal intercourse but through clitoral stimulation. Foreplay makes it much easier for them to climax, making them aroused. Their engines are cold and need time to warm up. Foreplay serves that purpose.

It should be done in a soft, tender, slow, and gen-tle manner. Make sure you don't hurt her as this will have the opposite effect to 'turning her on'.

Foreplay includes:

Kissing or nibbling her ear, kissing behind her ear lobe (very arousing for the woman.)

Kissing licking the base of her spine slowly and moving upward.

Gently rubbing and kissing her arms, stomach, legs, and back.

Stroking, caressing her legs including the calves, thighs, and under and upper side of the leg.

Kissing her neck, throat, side of the neck, back of the neck from behind, both of you standing with the man behind, squeezing her breasts rubbing her clitoris, and kissing her neck all at the same time.

Gently kissing licking, sucking, and gently biting her neck/breasts and nipples.

Moving your tongue slowly up and down against her nipple or in a circular fashion.

Whispering and talking dirty, telling her how sexy she is.

Kissing and licking her vagina.

Kissing her and sucking her tongue (gently).

Clitoral stimulation through gentle slow circular strokes or up and down.

Sensual massage all over her body. Kissing or licking her stomach.

Kissing the pubic bone area just above the vagina. Kissing her inner thighs, starting from the bottom making your way up to the inner part of her leg next to the vagina.

Teasing her by touching the outer part of her vagina with the head of your penis but not inserting it.

Whilst pulling her top off, pull it over her eyes and kiss her. Not being able to see you and what you're going to do is very arousing for her.

Dry sex. The man lies naked on top of woman whilst she has her knickers on and with his erect penis, he drives it into her. Doing this can quickly get her engine revved up.

Talking dirty, whispering dirty things into her ear. Sending her dirty SMS messages.

Foreplay with your man may include:

- Sensual Massage, with or without a lubricant

- Kissing and touching the upper thigh to lower belly. He reacts to your kisses and touches

- Sitting on his lap and aligning your private part with his.

- Whilst eating dinner together, rubbing your hand against his dick.

- Placing a mirror and the woman standing next to him without clothes on.

- The woman talking dirty.

- Gently stroking the underside of the man's penis.

- Stripping and dancing erotically

- Stroking his penis with your hands with his pants on.

- Stroking his penis with your foot under the table with his pants on whilst eating dinner.

During foreplay, don't spend too much time on one spot or, your woman will begin to feel bored.

Even during intercourse you can return to foreplay to heighten the pleasure for her and it will help you last longer in bed, too, as it will be a short break for you.

Take each piece of clothing off slowly, one at a time. Her top, socks, bra, underpants, etc.

Get olive oil put it on your woman's body chest, breasts, legs and stomach. Move your hand up and down slowly around her breasts, stomach, and sides of her stomach, giving her a massage.

It's a great turn on. Then, suck and kiss away at her breasts. Apply oil to her arms and legs, massaging slowly and gently, in a circular fashion followed by massaging her vagina licking and kissing it. Put on some sexy music in the background to turn her on even more.

Erotic massages are a great way to get your woman to relax and aroused for sex. Warning do not start massaging her sexually straightaway. Start without touching her sexual organs for at least 15 minutes. But remember you the woman should be wet always before he inserts his dick inside you. Otherwise your arousal levels will always be playing catch up with his.

3

GO REEEAL SLOW!

Do not rush because the woman (also) has needs

(which should be fulfilled).

Ever eaten a nice cake, slowly chewing as many times you could to make the pleasure of eating the cake last longer?

Men, apply this to your sex life!

A sliding penis going in and out slowly can be exhilarating for both of you as it gives you both enough time to enjoy the feeling. Don't just make the penetration time longer. Make the whole experience last longer from the starter meal, kissing, sexual talk, foreplay, caressing, and the main course, intercourse.

Go slowly and gently. This is more arousing than fast, rough, and hard, especially at the beginning. Going slowly will also dramatically increase the man's ability to last in bed.

Many men think fast, rough, and hard is great. Don't do this straight away. Slow is better for the both of you, especially at the beginning. Once you've built momentum then you can go fast. She'll tell you when she wants you to go hard and fast.

A lot of men have the idea in their head that going fast and hard is the way all the time.

It's not! Women are glass vessels, and as glass vessels, we need to be handled with gentle care. This goes for foreplay, too.

This is not a race. You should both try to enjoy the experience for as long as possible. The longer it lasts, the more enjoyable it is likely to be for the both of you.

Women can take eleven to thirty minutes to climax whilst men can take two and a half to three minutes.

The slower you go, the longer you'll last, and the longer it lasts, the more powerful the orgasm of both the man and woman is likely to be.

Many men don't realise this fact. They look for the short orgasm and pleasure but don't realise they are really missing out on more powerful orgasms by simply slowing down, lasting longer without climaxing, and giving and receiving foreplay.

A man can have orgasms without climaxing, too, just like women.

As a man, once you ejaculate, it's over. Why cut the pleasure to two to three minutes? Why not keep the pleasure of your penis rubbing against your woman's vagina going for much longer? The longer it goes on, the more likely you both are to enjoy it. The longer and more she enjoys it, the more she'll want to have sex with you in the future. In real estate the key word is location location location. Sex with women the key word is time time time. Giving her enough time for foreplay, enough time for stimulating her clitoris and enough time for intercourse until she is satisfied.

It's simple. Give her what she wants and she'll give you what you want.

Minimally, the man should aim to last at least thirty minutes engaged in sexual activity. That time includes foreplay. Of course, there is no maximum time. For some, it can go on for an hour or several hours even.

At the end of the day, women enjoy slow sex MORE than fast sex. Just ask her. Get your woman to rub your penis gently, slowly. Then, get her to rub it rough and hard. You'll see the former is more enjoyable than the latter as the latter is likely to hurt you and give you less pleasure than the former. The rule is, if you are going to go fast (late stages of sex), make sure you're not being too rough as this will kill her arousal, just as it will kill yours if she rubbed your penis too roughly.

4

BE A WILD ANIMAL
WITH HER!

Sometimes, a woman wants you, the man, to be a wild animal and not be the gentle prince. Gentle sex all the time can be boring. Spice it up with raunchy sex. Have sex with her as if it is the first time you've both met.

Kiss her fast, tear off her clothes, her shirt, her trousers, blouse, her bra, and underwear, and just throw her onto the bed. Devour her. Pound and pummel her vagina in the missionary position. She wants it!

5

BE A SLUT!

Many women want to behave seductively, erotically, with their men but fear their men will see them as "loose". This should not be the case. Dance for him erotically, he should love you more for making the effort to please him. People have affairs because it's new, exciting, sexy, offering them something different than their spouse is offering. If he/she is getting their desires and fantasies fulfilled in bed with you, there's no reason for them to look to someone else to give them amazing sex.

Don't always see your woman in the same way. See her as your mistress, your sex friend. This goes for the woman, too. Be as saucy, and dirty as you both can be toward each other. Learn to flirt and seduce each other.

Here are a few seduction techniques Steve uses on me.

- He listens to me when I feel overwhelmed and stressed. He shows me empathy. Remember ever watching movies the first guy who the girl talks to when she's stressed she starts kissing as he listens and shows empathy. The trick is to listen and let her make the decision.

- Steve has squeezed my nipples between two fingers and starting making circles with them. Next thing I want is for him to kiss and suck them and finally slide his cock inside me.

- Many times Steve will turn to me and say, "let me see if I can get you horny by touching you." He'll pretend as if he does not want sex. Once he's got me horny and pushes me away saying he does not want it, the more he makes me want it. We've had sex in my mother's living room, three different bedrooms at my friend's house because of him not being "interested." We always want what we can't have. Hence why women want married men.

- Talk to your woman and say hey if you're not in the mood for sex let me just pleasure you. Make it clear it's about her receiving pleasure. What woman would refuse receiving pleasure? Many times women say they're not in the mood because the man needs to create the mood. You could start by sitting and kissing her shoulder blades, ear lobes, talking about her day whilst you do this. Kiss her neck. Steve gets me in the mood for sex within ten minutes sometimes after the massage he gives me using olive oil. Massage her shoulder blades and back. Become skilled at giving massages.

6

THINK DIRTY,
TALK DIRTY,
BE DIRTY!

Men love dirty talk. Why'd you think there are sex chat up lines with many customers being men? Most men are moved by sexual moans and sighs and the slow, heavy breathing of women. As a woman, become comfortable with a few oohs and aahs. Sexual talk will really light the fire of desire. use it.

To talk dirty to your woman, describe what you want to do to her rather than what you want her to do to you. You could initiate things by sending SMS messages, describing what you want to do when you see her. "Caress", "thrust", and "make love" is great for women. Or, "I wanna get on top of you" and "........

I wanna lick/ suck ...." is more arousing as she will picture the act with you beforehand. Wouldn't it be great, having her or him picturing having sex with you? During sex, say each other's names with moans.

Or, talk about what you're gonna do to her different body parts explicitly. Make your voice sexy, deepening it a little for her. Be as sexually explicit as you can. Be really as sexually rude, explicit, and naughty with each other. Dirty talk during sex is one of the fastest ways to really make the sex steamy. Use X rated vocabulary. Enjoy it, embrace it. Keep it alive with great dirty talk. Below are a few things to say to her whilst inside her. Ask her questions that she'll automatically say yes to they are incredibly powerful! Also here's an idea. Learn to talk dirty in French with a sexy accent.

Women find multi lingual men more attractive.

- I'm gonna ram you with my wet hard dick

- Can you feel my wet warm hard cock/dick inside you?

- Wana feel what my hard dick feels like inside you? (ask this just before sex whilst kissing)

- You like that? Yeah? You like my dick inside you? (Ask this when you know she's really starting to enjoy whatever you're doing to her.

- If this feels amazing imagine what I'll do to you bent over.

- I'm gonna make your cum flow like the river Nile.

- I'm gonna FUCK the innocence out of you!

- Do you wana feel my juice inside you?/Feeeel my juice.

- I'm gonna make you squirt like a water fountain.

- I'm gonna fuck your brains out!

- I'm gonna pummel you, until your cum starts dripping down your pussy and all over the bed.

7

THE GREATEST OPPORTUNITY TO ENJOY SEX!

For some reason, many people become dirty, naughty, outside relationships.

Have your dirty, erotic desires and fantasies fulfilled Do all the things people do in affairs.

- Call each other by different names Jack, Ryan (sexy names women love and Cindy. Role play an affair.

- Go on an erotic vacation.

- Send erotic text messages to each other during work lunch break.

- Always dress and smell sexy as if you're meeting each other for the first time for an affair. This keeps things fresh.

- Meet each other in a restaurant and touch each other's genitals under the table.

- Meet at different locations don't go together as people having affairs meet at the agreed location and time. For example swimming pools engage in hot kissing and touching, spa, hotel rooms, in your office.

8

GIVE HER GREAT SERVICE AND SHE'LL KEEP BUYING!

If you had a product or a service you did not like, then you'd most likely want your money back, exchange it, or, get the product or service from someplace else, right? Women want great sex. Your woman is no different. Give her great sex! And she'll want more and more. As a man, you won't have to try and convince her to have sex with you. She'll initiate sex. Otherwise, sex becomes a chore 'cos you're such a bore. Giving her great sex is to door to more sex. Sorry for the lame rhyme, but it's true. Don't you men forget it! A lot of men complain they don't have enough sex. Increasing the quality of sex for women will likely lead to an increase in the number of times you have sex each week. Focus on increasing the quality of sex and the quantity will increase. In other words, the more you please her the more she'll spread her legs for you.

If you're not involved in a long term relationship. You'll build a reputation for being an amazing guy in bed amongst women.

9

FIND HER EROGENEOUS ZONES

There are certain parts of a woman's body, which, if touched, caressed, sucked, or kissed properly, will turn her on.

These are:

1. The nape of the neck or back of the neck. Kiss and nibble her neck. Kissing her neck from behind, including the back of the neck and squeezing her breasts, moving them in a rhythmic circular motion can be very arousing. The man could press his penis against her buttocks and run his hands up her inner thighs.

2. Spine. Many women love having their men's tongue run down their spine and have the end of the spine area kissed and caressed.

3. Back of the knees.

4. Buttocks. The man should squeeze and caress these during intercourse, not just during foreplay, by grabbing her buttocks, spreading his fingers wide, and squeezing both of them firmly

5. Inner thigh. Slowly running his hand up this region can really arouse her.

6. Clitoris. The man can expose her clitoris by spreading the lips of the vagina and gently pulling back her hood, then use your middle finger pad and make circular movements, side to side or up and down. Be very very gentle, like you're stroking her with a feather. Do it at a slow, gentle, consistent speed. This

applies to kissing, too. This can be a real turn on and can lead a woman to have a clitoral orgasm. Use olive oil or any lubricant to add smoothness and reduce friction, which can cause pain. It'll add to her pleasure, too.

7. The man should take the clitoris in his mouth and kiss, lick, suck on it gently. This should be done lightly and harder if she wants it.

8. Breasts. The man can suck kiss, lick, and nibble the nipples. He should squeeze, caress, and suck these during intercourse. This can be done slowly. He could lick the tip of the nipple, too using the tip of his tongue.

9. Hold one firmly even and do the above.

10. Lips. Kissing can be a very arousing for both the woman and man.

11. Kissing her vagina

10

WOMEN HAVE
ERECTIONS LIKE MEN!

Did you know your women's clitoris becomes erect just like your penis? A woman's clitoris is made up of the same erectile tissue as men's penises. Through dirty words, foreplay, clitoral stimulation, or with the stimulation of the vagina through the insertion of your finger, the clitoris should become erect. When it does, once the penis is inserted, the pleasure of your woman and yours will be heightened dramatically. GET HER HARD AND ERECT NOW!

11

STIMULATE HER IN MORE WAYS THAN ONE!

Just because you're penetrating her vagina does not mean that's the end. Maybe you, the man, could stimulate her clitoris whilst simultaneously giving her pleasure with the insertion of your penis. Insert your penis into her vagina from behind and stimulate her clitoris with your right middle finger using olive oil to reduce friction, with the other hand squeezing her breasts and buttocks, and kiss her neck, all at the same time. This way, she is getting pleasure in four ways!

In the missionary position, you could insert your penis into her vagina and kiss one breast whilst rubbing and squeezing the other. You could both stand with you, the man, entering her from behind. Now, penetrate her, give her clitoral stimulation with one hand, kiss her on the neck and earlobes, turn her head and kiss her lips, squeeze her breasts and buttocks, with the other hand, and talk dirty into her ear. Now, she gets your penis, clitoral stimulation with one hand, kisses on her neck and her lips, breast and buttock stimulation with the other hand, AND sexual dirty talk in her ear.

That's various different ways she's getting pleasure all at the same time. AMAZING SEX, ISN'T IT? Men must multitask during sex.

12

HAVE HOT SHOWERS AND BATHE TOGETHER, BEFORE AND AFTER SEX

Have a shower before engaging in sex. This will make you both more easily aroused and energetic. You will both be much more easily responsive during foreplay as it will awaken your senses.

Why not have a shower together after sex as well? It'll strengthen your bond and intimacy. If your other half is in the shower, quietly sneak in and join them. You could kiss and touch each other anywhere; very sexy indeed! Be playful, throw water at each other. It'll reinvigorate you for more sex, too. You could bathe together in the tub. The hot water on your bodies and seeing and touching each other's naked bodies is very sexy.

13

MUTUALLY MASTURBATE EACHOTHER!

Whilst standing facing and kissing each other, using olive oil on your finger tips, you could gently rub each other's genitals.

Kiss her neck from behind and touch and stimulate her clitoris. She could rub your penis from the front, standing.

Move to the bed whilst continuing to kiss each other, kneel on your knees, and carry on the mutual masturbation.

She could get on top of you, with her backside facing your face, and lick your genitals and you could do the same to her licking her pussy.

14

GRIND HER SHE'LL LOVE IT!

When your woman gets on top of you, what does she do? Grind you, right? Why? Coz this causes your penis to touch her pleasure button, her clitoris. By getting on top, you could move forward toward his chest with your breasts touching his. This should give you more clitoral contact.

The man in missionary could shift his weight forward, which will cause his pubic bone to be on top of hers and touching. For mind blowing pleasure for the woman, have her close her legs and keep them together.

The man enters her first, then she closes her legs, and he moves his legs to either side of her legs. This position is called the coital alignment.

This will narrow the walls of her vagina and both of you will experience greater rubbing of the penis and clitoris. The key is to get your penis to touch her clitoris. Gentle thrusts are enough to get her going. This means as the man, you can last longer and easily. You don't need to pummel her a hundred times as a few rubs against her clitoris will set her off wildly. I'll say it again. Men you don't need to pound our vaginas a hundred times to get us to orgasm.

15

CHANGE THE PLACE
YOU HAVE SEX!

Sometimes, sex on the same bed can become rather dry. Spice it up. Do it in another bedroom, the living room, on the sofa, on a chair. The woman could sit on the sofa with her legs dangling in the air whilst the man penetrates her. Or, the man could sit and his woman could enter him with her back to him as if she is sitting down on the sofa.

Try the kitchen table, against a wall facing each other, or with the woman's back to her man, or in the bathroom or on the floor.

What about on a water bed, or on a yoga ball?

Hire out a caravan for a weekend for sex. Book a room in a hotel.

Why not in the countryside in the fields, in a tent?

What about in water? As a result of no gravity, the man could easily lift his woman off the ground and have sex standing with her in a hugging position and her legs curled up wrapped around him.

The key to great sex is to not be afraid to practice and try different things, even if you don't get it right the first time. The wrong thing to do is to keep doing the same things over and over again and expect different results and then wonder why sex is so boring and routine. Below are some places you could have sex.

- Pool

- CAR with mattress check out fuway car mattress on Amazon

- Caravan holiday

- Tent

- Skinny dip and have sex

- On a Sofa bed

- Hotel balcony

- Living room floor use sofa cushions to make a bed.

- House bathroom

- Hire an office space and do it

- Open Field in the countryside

- Changing room at retail store just tell the assistant that you're checking if your girlfriend is ok.

- Public Park climb over after closing time and get to it. Take bed sheet to spread onto the grass.

- In the back of a limo

- In a bouncy castle.

- On a trampoline

- On a bean bag chair it's great for doggy

- In a overnight train sleeping compartment

- On a washing machine his penis becomes a life size vibrator

- Indoor Sex swing (check it out on Amazon

- On a strong massage bed

- On a water bed

- On the dining table

Make a list of sex goals of different places and countries you wana have sex. So far I've had sex.

- In a Shanghai hotel

- In a Turkish waterpark

- In a Turkish hotel lift

- On my best friend's living room sofa

- At a park after closing time. We took bed sheets of course.

- At a lingerie shop changing room

- Three bedrooms at my moms.

- At a kids park swing after closing time

- Pretending to argue on a plane and following Steve into the toilet and having sex there whilst pretending to argue.

- In the woods

Sex goals are amazing at keeping things fresh. Sex goals can be different positions, different role plays, different sexual techniques as well as places and countries. Write down yours for the new year.

My Sex goals for 2017 are

- In the back of a van with a bed inside.

- At my friend's farm

- In a barn

- On a erotic holiday pool

- At a sex theme park

- Holding my body off the floor by putting my feet against wall and letting Steve drill me.

- On a boat

- On a shore where the water meets the sand like Kelly Brook in survival island

- Playing twister naked

- Recording and creating a sex video album of all the times we had sex during 2017.

16

GOOD SMELLS TURNS WOMEN ON

Bad smells are always a major turn off. So before kissing after a long day's work, take a shower and have some minted gum. Men you should always make yourselves smell nice before having sex with their women. It's a real turn on for women. Also, don't forget to shave your pubic hairs. Make sure the hair does not prickle her. Women love clean shaven cocks, and balls.

17

PLAY A GAME

Get twelve pieces of paper. The woman gets six you get six. On each, you each write down six sex acts you want the other person to do to you. Don't tell your partner what they are.

Then, place the two groups of cards in two circles on the floor with the blank side facing up. You could toss a coin to decide who spins first. If the man goes first, he spins a bottle in the girl's circle of cards and does what the cards says. You could add more paper to add more sex acts and excitement. Whatever the card tells you to do you must do. Download a sex dice app. Edit and add your own sex acts in. The partner roles the dice on their phone and the dice tells them what to do. You have to listen to the dice.

Lie in bed naked together and take it in turns to try and seduce one another to have sex. Each partner could have an allotted time to try and seduce their spouse. The seduction can involve stimulating any part of the body the seducer wants to touch, saying whatever they want. The one being seduced must try and resist. The loser is the one who gives in, ending up wanting to have sex.

One game me and Steve love to play is, he is a priest and I'm a young nun who has come for an assessment to join the establishment. I must prove my piety by resisting whatever Steve does to me to arouse my sexual desires. Just like above Spin the bottle is played except with just one circle of cards having sex acts written on the other side which is facing the floor.

Below are examples

1. Lick/suck her tits – 1 minute

2. Kiss her neck from behind squeeze her breasts whispering dirty things into her ear. E.g you are weak I'm gonna slide my dick inside you. 1 minute

3. Cover her tits in Nutella chocolate lick and suck it off slowly.

4. Stick your finger into her vagina and massage it.

5. Rub/lick her clitoris in circles write the alphabet on her clitoris with tongue   – 2 minutes

6. Massage both sides of her vulva – 2 minutes (refer to chapter how to get her really wet.)

7. Whilst standing rub your the head of your penis against her vagina and clitoris – 1 minute

8. Kiss & masturbate – 1 minute

9. Blindfold her for rest of session and do what you want with her

As a nun, I fail and can't resist my sexual urges this game makes me so wet pouring with my juice dripping down my legs. And because I'm so aroused it doesn't take long for me to orgasm or cave in and force Steve's dick inside me.

18

SIN IS IN

You could role-play as well. One spouse plays the role of the innocent, loyal already married spouse not wanting to have sex. The other spouse the hungry horny, sinful person trying to seduce and overcome the resistance put up by the innocent, loyal one. Change roles. One day, it's the woman, who is the hungry one and another day, it's the man. In the end, eventually, the resistance always fails and the loyal one gives in to the dirty one and you end up having a raunchy sexual affair. This is amazing. Women tend to be the ones who have more control over their   sexual desires than men. Here, they can eventually lose control to their desires. Act slutty without the fear of being judged and be their sexual selves with no barriers

Act as a professional adult tutor, either the man is the tutor or the woman. The other partner plays the adult student. The roles can change, depending on the preference. One thing leads to another. You could be praying together as brother and sister in faith. You find each other attractive and start talking to each other, going out together, flirting. She invites you into her house and you know the rest.

Other scenarios:

1. Doctor/patient

2. Adult teacher/adult student in class

3. Skilled manual worker and home alone female customer.

4. Airport security. You tell her she needs to take off her clothes for "security" reasons. She gets strip searched.

5. Role play colleagues at office together and you both lose control. Make the table your office desk and have sex.

6. Your children are not home. The guy is their tutor. The woman, a home alone wife. He asks for a "quick few" minutes to discuss their progress.

7. Be the gentlemen who is just dropping a woman home late at night after a night out. Her house is far away. At her door, she feels bad letting you go back by yourself so late in the rain . She allows you to stay and sleep at her house. At first, you refuse but eventually give in. You sleep on the floor but she's kind enough eventually to allow you to share her bed. But you put pillows between yourselves as a barrier between the two of you. You talk, getting to know each other more. Eventually, you both "fall" into sin.

19

SHORT BREAKS FROM EACHOTHER AND NO SEX CAN REVITALIZE THE RELATIONSHIP!

Sometimes too much sex is too much. Maybe your woman could have a sleepover with her friends for a day or two, spend a week at her family house. The distance could bring you two closer. This'll recreate hunger for each other.

20

TOUCH HER HEART AND SHE'LL LET YOU TOUCH HER VAGINA!

Men and women truly are opposite. Many men think they can always have sex with their women by touching them sexually, such as touching their breasts, and down below all the time. That's not the case!

Women fall into sex through romance. So, if you wanna have sex: Take her for a night walk. Take her to a romantic dinner. Date your woman! Give her a flower a week.

That's better than giving her fifty once a year. The best of actions are those that are done on a consistent basis. Think about your life. Going to the gym is not rewarding and beneficial for you once every blue moon as going once a week, now is it?

Be consistently being romantic with your woman through kind, romantic words about her beauty. Use rhetoric such as 'Your eyes are like pearls.' If you find it hard as you've never been romantic or are not the romantic type, send SMS messages with love messages. Show her you care for her and not just her body for mere sex.

Hold her in your arms, hug her. This is a HUGE DEAL for women. Women love hugging and cuddling up. Ever wonder why some single women like to snuggle up to a teddy bear at night?

Sit on a tree with your back supported and she sits with her back and head against you. Lie on grass in a park together, holding hands, and look at the sky. Go walk on a beach. Hold her hand and kiss her. Women become annoyed and angry at the smallest things but they also appreciate the smallest of kindnesses, too. Use it to your advantage. Oh, men, rock her heart and then you can rock her in bed. BUT, make sure you rock her in bed, too.

21

MAKE NOISE WHEN HE/SHE PLEASES YOU

This goes both ways. As long as it is real and not fake, it's great feedback for the other party as they know they are doing things right. You'll please each other more and enjoy each other more. Release your voice and be loud. It can make sex simply mind-blowing as opposed to stifling and suppressing your voice and keeping things down. Relax. Make sexual moans of delight and scream. Get sound proofing in your room and house if you fear others will hear. Play something loud like an action movie on your iPad to block out the sound. Just make sure you release your voice and cry moans of delight during sex. It could be the x-factor for average sex and amazing sex.

22

(I) GO TO THE SHALLOWEND

Take your penis and enter just the head of it at the entrance of her vagina in and out real fast. The good news is the man won't feel much sensation which means he can do it without Cumming. But for her, it's amazing. One of the most sensitive sexually responsive parts of your woman's vagina is located at the entrance. Go in and out with just the head of your penis at the entrance real fast in missionary position and it should make her wet. Do this regularly and she should pour out with her own cum. You can keep doing this and she should gush with her own water. She'll be a very satisfied customer. Remember, the **outer third** of your woman's vagina is the most sensitive, NOT the deep, inner part as many people think. It's a great way to get her going crazy fast and also the man can last long as it's only the head of the penis going in and out.

23

(II) GO TO THE SHALLOW END

Take the head of your penis. Apply lubricant. Then, rub the outer parts of your woman's vagina. Hold the base of your penis and vibrate your penis head against the outer parts of your woman's vagina. Vibrate it especially against her clitoris.

24

VARIETY IS THE SPICE OF LIFE

Changing sexual positions and sexual techniques will make your woman's desire skyrocket. It will in-crease the chances of her climaxing. So do it. Don't stick to the missionary position and think that's enough for her. It's not! Mix it up! There are literally over hundreds and hundreds of different sex positions. Learn them and apply them. Making mistakes is fine. Experimenting will be fun and different than the mundane missionary position.

25

ALLOW HER AROUSAL TO FLOW THROUGH HER BODY

Use kisses and tenderness to increase her arousal gradually. DON'T try to give her five minutes of pleasure as her arousal will be limited to just her genital area. Women take longer. Let her arousal flow through her body. The tortoise wins the race, not the rabbit. Give her time to gradually build up her arousal.

26

KISS AND CARESS
HER ALL OVER

Don't just kiss and caress her genitals. Kiss and caress her everywhere. And I mean, everywhere.

Kiss as many different parts of her body as possible. Kiss her arms, legs, back, and stomach. Gently touching, stroking, sucking, and licking your woman's neck, back, stomach, nipples, thighs, vagina, and clitoris are enough sometimes to cause an orgasm.

27

COMPLIMENT HER BODY DURING SEX

Women are generally insecure about their weight and their looks. They are even more so when naked in the bedroom. That's why they turn off the lights. Compliment her beauty. Don't say 'these breasts are...' Say, 'your breasts are.' Adding the your is the x-factor to reducing her insecurities. Adding the your will make her feel sexy about her body.

Make it clear how attractive you find her. She needs to know.

28

PLAY WITH HER BREASTS

Playing with her nipples and gently sucking her nipples and breasts can make the vagina wet and ready for intercourse. Only enter woman's vagina when she is fully wet and ready for you. Ask her to tell you when she's wet. It's the most obvious way to know if she's been fully aroused by you or not. Only then do you enter her with your penis. Here's a trick.

The man should put olive oil on his penis. Then in the missionary position let her guide his penis in. This way she is in control. The man should do nothing. Let her move from left to right guiding the penis in gradually. The man needs to merely remain still she could shake her ass under him in the missionary position. She could even move her ass up and down so now she is fucking him even though he is the one on top remaining still.

29

USE A MIRROR DURING SEX

If you don't have a mirror, where you can see what you're doing to each other during sex, on the bed or elsewhere, then it's time to get one. It'll be incredibly arousing for the both of you. Having a full length view and being able to see what you're doing to each other in bed really is very sexy. Imagine he's fondling your breasts from behind and kissing you on your neck whilst you can feel his penis pressed against your buttocks. All of this is in full view in front of a mirror. What if you could see each other in missionary position entering in and out of each other? What if you, the woman, could see your man entering you from behind or from a side view? GET A MIRROR NOW!

30

EAT EGGS TO PRODUCE HARDER AND FASTER ERECTIONS

The more firm or harder man's erections are, the more pleasure for the both of you. The man should eat eggs as they will not only give him this, but they'll give him more regular erections, too. And after ejaculating, he'll get an erection faster to give her more pleasure. Eat two eggs a day.

31

HOW TO GET LONG, HARD ERECTIONS

The more regular erections the man has, the harder his erections are likely to be. Each time he has an erection, he is exercising the smooth muscles responsible for producing erections.

Lack of sex will lead to weaker erections.

Every day, get olive oil and with your left hand, rub your hand onto your penis up and down slowly. Start from the base of your penis and rub all the way up to the top slowly and consistently. Contract your PC muscles if you want to increase the blood flow, further making your erection extremely hard. Keep rubbing and bring yourself to near ejaculation. BUT DON'T! Let yourself and your desire subside for ten second when you reach this point. Then, when your desire to ejaculate has subsided, begin rubbing again. Rub yourself again, reaching the point of ejaculating then stopping and starting again. This will train your mind and penis to not ejaculate too quickly and train you to have greater control over your ejaculation muscles. Use a mirror to see yourself from a side view, if needed. You could stand and do this. Or, lie on a bed. Your woman can do this for you.

Doing this exercise, called edging, every day for twenty minutes will:

1. Increase the firmness and hardness of your erections. It can make your erections and penis extremely hard, giving you and your woman more pleasure during intercourse.

2. It will strengthen your ability to control yourself from not ejaculating too early during intercourse.

3. Great remedy for erectile dysfunction.

4. Increases sexual stamina.

5. Remedy for premature ejaculation as it will desensitize you.

6. It helps you develop a harder, larger, and healthier penis.

7. It allows you to reach your peak hardness for a larger amount of time.

8. Allows you to discover dry orgasm during intercourse after a few months.

32

AROUSE HER WITH
YOUR BEHAVIOUR

Men are turned on by women's appearance. Women are turned on more through how you behave and make her feel. Turn your attention to how you make her feel. Make her feel beautiful, precious, and protected. If you wanna turn her on in bed, behave very manly. Maybe deepen your voice a little, too. Take control in bed.

33

SLEEP NAKED TOGETHER

Don't put your clothes back on after sex.

Keep them off. Sleep naked together. Make sure your naked bodies are touching. The man could sleep with his arms around his woman. If it's not comfortable, do it until she falls asleep. Alternatively, she could place her head onto his chest whilst naked and nod off. The feeling of sleeping with nothing on is very powerful.

34

WEAR SEXY LINGERIE

Drive him wild with desire. Invest in some sexy lingerie. Be as kinky as you can. The woman should want her man's eyes on her and vice versa. Make him go crazy. Go and get some lingerie from Victoria's Secret. Why not dress up in an exotic black arab niqaab with transparent abaya and have sex in it? Or, in a sexy thong. Look around, shop around. Be as sexually provocative as you can be.

35

RE -ENACT YOUR
WEDDING NIGHT

If you're married, put on your wedding clothes and role play your wedding night. Make it as real as possible as if you're in the bedroom together for the first time. Do the normal things such as the husband offering a drink, Have a conversation as if you are getting to know each other more for the first time. This is a great chance to right the things that may have gone wrong on the wedding night, if any.

36

MAKE A MOVIE

Wouldn't it be great to record everything the guy sees when he has sex with his woman? So when he sees his penis enter her vagina it's recorded as he sees it. Or how she spreads her legs, bends over, when she gets on top of him. Get a universal head mount for your smartphone. So you can place your Iphone on your forehead and record her facial expressions as you the man hover over her in a missionary position. Whatever you turn your eyes and head to that's what will be recorded. So imagine being able to record the man's view of doggy style? Being able to see her ass and your dick again and again. Her sexy voice as she screams the house down as you pummel her vagina in any position. Her juice pouring out of her vagina like a river bursting through a river bank.

37

USE LUBRICANTS

If you wanna make your sex sensual and amazing, adding a lubricant like olive oil really can make all the difference. The man could place some on the head of penis and enter his woman. Don't put too much or it will be too slippery and have the opposite effect. It'll make entering the woman painless for her as the man's penis will simply slide right in. KY jelly is an excellent lubricant and can help your woman climax faster.

38

THE FASTEST WAY FOR
HER TO HAVE AN ORGASM

The woman should get on top, with her man lying on his back. She should lean back, resting her hands on the bed behind herself. Or lean forward, resting her hands above his head. The angle created will increase clitoral stimulation. The woman should grind her man's penis. This position is one of the fastest ways for the woman to achieve orgasm. In fact, women on top positions are the fastest way for women to achieve orgasms. The man should place his hands under his head, lying relaxed. If the man is afraid he will ejaculate, he should, from the beginning, breathe slowly and deeply, and keep his sexual emotions under control. It may be best to not express them until after the woman has achieved her big O. This means no sounds such as groaning. Keep quiet and focus on her pleasure.

If you find yourself, as a woman, not having an orgasm, get on top and grind him. In this position, he could squeeze your breasts, talk very dirty to you, squeeze your buttocks with spread fingers, and run his hands up your legs. The woman should grind him slowly at first, building up momentum. She could bring herself to orgasm this way. Or, she could go really fast rubbing her clitoris hard against his penis. Try different positions. Bounce up and down your man. Grind him chest to chest with her breasts touching his chest. She could arch back, supporting her hands on the bed or on his thighs. Try the reverse cowgirl position.

Women on top positions are great because the woman is now in control of her pleasure, thus making it easy for her to achieve orgasm because of her clitoris being stimulated directly by his cock. Lean forward for greater clitoral stimulation placing hands besides his head

39

WAYS FOR HIM TO
LAST LONGER IN BED

There's nothing more annoying for a woman to go through taking off her clothes, looking forward to having her sexual desires fulfilled, than her man ejaculating within a few minutes after commencing sex. If this problem persists regularly, it can have serious ramifications on both the man's and woman's sex life and, ultimately, their relationship.

So how does the man prevent himself from ejaculating too fast and early?

1. Have sex more regularly. Studies have shown men who have more regular sex last longer in bed. The simple reason being, the longer a man goes without sex, the more easily excited and stimulated he becomes to sexual stimuli, which makes it easier for him to ejaculate and harder for him to last longer.

2. Penetrate her with the head of your penis. Don't penetrate your woman with your frenulum part of your penis. Certainly not at the beginning. Penetrating her with your frenulum part of your penis is the part that will send you to ejaculate early. It's the part that gets most excited easily and quickly. Don't forget the front part of the vagina is the most sexually excited part so penetrating her with your head and not ejaculating early works well. Whilst going in and out of her rub her vagina with the upper side part of your penis and NOT the frenulum side. This means you're also more likely to rub her clitoris too. Go reeeal slow and rub against her clit hard. She should get really horny and wild within a few minutes.

3. Control his emotions and voice sounds. During sex, you, the man, should control your emotions and not focus on getting pleasure. Don't make grunts or any sexual sounds. Stay calm. This will prevent you from getting too excited too quickly.

4. Make him ejaculate once before sex. Why not give him a hand job and make him ejaculate? When he's ready with another erection, then have sex with him. The second time around, it will be harder and take greater sexual stimulation and time for him to ejaculate. In other words, he'll last longer in bed.

5. Avoid dirty talk. If talking dirty to your man will push him over the edge then stop and withhold your voice and tongue. Just moan and groan instead.

6. Breathe longer and deeper. This is a simple fact. The more aroused you, the man, become, the shorter and faster your breaths become. If you find yourself becoming too excited too fast, breathe slow and deep. If nothing else, works try this.

7. Remain still. If you, the man, find yourself on the verge of ejaculating, pull yourself calmly out of your woman and become totally still without moving for eight to ten seconds. If some positions, such as the missionary, get you too excited too fast, change positions or penetrate your woman slowly.

8. Stop start technique. Once the man feels too aroused and he is getting to close to climaxing, he should pause for a period lasting between 5-10 seconds until his arousal subsides. He should repeat this technique for as long as is needed. A man may feel he needs to be manly and not stop and continue to pummel her. But if she knows you're stopping to last for her she'll appreciate it and see you're not selfish.

9. Squeeze technique. When he feels he is getting close, he should stop stimulation and squeeze right below the head of the penis, focussing on the urethra, which is on the underside of the penis.

10. Use a desensitizing condom. The downside to using a condom, of course, is it can make the pleasure less intense for

both the man and the woman and cannot be compared to skin to skin contact.

11. Use blind fold and ear plugs. Why? Men are aroused by what they can see AND hear. By blocking the seeing and hearing of a woman that should increase his ability to last.

12. If all else fails then there is a quick fast step for man to last longer. Use stud 100. It's a penis desensitization spray that reduces the penis sensitivity to sexual touches with the woman's vagina. The man should use it on the under-side part of the penis (frenulum) just under the head. As that is the most sensitive part of the penis that causes ejaculations. No intercourse should take place for at least ten minutes to allow time for the spray to work

Try and use all the techniques above, especially steps one to five. Step ten is the easiest fastest and most effective method to delay ejaculations.

FIVE REASONS WHY MEN CUM TOO FAST!

If still the above does not work here are the **five** main reasons men come too fast.

1.Flexing your PC muscle

This is the muscle you use to stop yourself from pissing now and holding it in. Never contract your PC muscle early into intercourse. This creates pressure on your penis and your body will want a release from the pressure so you'll come FAST. Keep your PC muscles relaxed for as long as you can. Do PC muscle and edging exercises to gain better control of when you ejaculate. Keep your PC muscles relaxed for as long as you can.

2.Holding your breath

Think about the last time you came and you'll realize you came and ejaculated when you held your breath. By holding your breath you'll once again create pressure on your body which your body looks to release through an ejaculation. Many of us have developed a habit of shallow breathing. Just make sure during sex you're taking deep slow breaths.

3.Closing your eyes

When you close your eyes there's only one thing you can focus on. The pleasure of your penis. The more you focus the harder it becomes to last.

4.Masturbation NEVER and I mean never masturbate for a few minutes this is a disaster. You are only training yourself to last for a few minutes when it comes to actual sex. Masturbate for at least ten minutes or more. Bring yourself to the point of ejaculation at least three four times during each session and you'll have better control over when you ejaculate. This is called edging. Also the woman should never give quick one minute to two minute hand jobs.

5. Lower your excitement level

When you the man have sex for the first ten minutes, do not show much emotion or groaning in fact if you can as my husband does act like a robot with a emotionless face. Someone who is there to serve the sexual needs of his woman first. Getting too excited too fast at the beginning will only lead to you coming way too soon.

Every time you have sex implement step one, two, and five at the same time you should be able to control yourself more.

Go slow because the slower you go the longer you'll last.

MEN CAN'T MULTI- TASK

One evening me and Steve were watching TV. I sat between his legs on the sofa he started caressing me soon we were having sex. But whilst he pummelled my vagina hard and fast he was watching the T.V instead of looking down at me. It worked like magic. He was so distracted by what was going on the T.V he remained horny enough to bang me for forty minutes non stop until I climaxed. Steve did not even ejaculate during that session.

I was so drained from that orgasm. If your man comes too fast try putting on a movie during sex on a phone or T.V. We women complain about how our men are so glued to the T.V all day right? Well, why not use it to get your orgasm?

Men cannot multi—task so since Steve's mind was fully focussed on the T.V. Around every twenty seconds he would look down at me as he pounded me just to get enough stimulation to stay erect. Warning this requires your man to be physically fit to be able to go at it non- stop for this long.

40

DO PC MUSCLE EXERCISES

Have you ever wanted to really urinate but had to hold it? That muscle you use to hold your urination is called the PC (Pubococcygeus muscle). It's also the muscle responsible for allowing the flow of urine out the man's penis or the woman's vagina. It also contracts during an orgasm.

By holding and squeezing the muscle every day, twenty times, the man can strengthen this muscle, which, in turn, will give him greater control to prevent himself from climaxing too early.

After birth, the woman's pleasurable as when the first time the couple engaged in sex, when it was tight. By exercising this muscle, she can tighten her vagina.

During intercourse, if the woman squeezes this muscle it will narrow the walls of her vagina, causing it to tighten on her man's penis, thus increasing the pleasure for both.

41

MAKE YOUR WOMAN
EJACULATE!

Insert two fingers slowly inside your woman's vagina with the palm facing up. Clip your nails and apply olive oil on your hand and her vagina before-hand or you'll hurt her. The lubricant will allow your fingers to slide in easily. Move inside in a snail like manner. Don't twist your finger or you'll seriously hurt her. Once inside, your finger should touch a firm wall in her vagina, motion your fingers in a "come here" gesture, as if you are summoning someone to yourself. Keep going. Keep motioning. It should become sooooo intense that she should wanna scratch you or hurt you. At one point, she will say, "I need to urinate." Assure her she does not but is on the verge of ejaculating. Have another bed sheet on the bed because she may squirt like a water fountain. This single act, done slowly, will create a mind blowing orgasm for the woman. She'll love you and will want to have sex with you if you finger her correctly. For a virgin woman, just insert your forefinger. Her vagina will still be very tight. One finger should be enough to not cause her any pain.

42

AGAIN! IT'S IN YOUR BEST INTERESTS TO FUIFILL YOUR WOMAN'S SEXUAL DESIRES

Many selfish men only think about themselves when it comes to sex. They just quickly, like an animal, fulfil their desires and stop, leaving the woman sexually unfulfilled.

An unfulfilled sex life can cause a woman to see the man as selfish and he is using her for only himself. It can cause her to hate him.

A lot of men just reach their climax and disengage, leaving their women frustrated.

It has been said, Give people what they want and you will get what you want."

Another quote: "Give and you will receive."

If a man is not satisfying his woman sexually, why is it a surprise to him that she makes excuses such as, 'I'm not in the mood' or 'I have a headache.'?

Imagine you did something for someone, knowing you were not going to get any benefit out of it, whether it be spiritual or material. Would you be motivated to do it?

If the woman knows she is not going to get anything except pain and unfulfilled desires then why should she have sex with you?

She gives and gives and gets nothing back!

However, reverse the situation. What if the man did fulfil her desires? What would happen then?

It's very likely she will be very motivated to engage in intercourse with her man almost every time he wants it.

Every time, she will anticipate and can't wait to enjoy the pleasure that she will surely receive and will more than readily have intercourse with her man.

It's pretty simple really.

When we enjoy doing something or had a good experience with something, we want to do it again.

If a customer has had a bad experience at a particular shop, would they want to go back there again?

Conversely, if the same customer had a good, enjoyable shopping experience at another shop, would they want to return and buy from there again?

It is very likely they would.

If the sexual experience for the woman is not good, she is more than likely to not want to repeat it and do it again. Unfortunately, a lot of women find sex painful, frustrating, and unfulfilling.

And unlike customer service, there is no customer service manager they can lodge a complaint to.

Some women are pushed to have their desires fulfilled with other men. But a massive part of the blame has to fall on the man.

43

IF YOUR WOMAN IS A VIRGIN

Don't be an animal and just jump on her. Talk to her. She is not a piece of flesh. Make her laugh. The more she laughs, the more relaxed she will be, and the more relaxed she becomes, the more receptive and easier she becomes to sex.

Give her a rose. Use romantic words. Before commencing sex, don't forget to:

- Use perfume, etc.

- Remove bad mouth and body odour.

- Dress attractively. Obviously beauty attracts ugliness repels.

- Shave pubic and underarm hair.

- Turn your mobile phone off. A phone ringing during sex can really kill the mood and spoil it for the both of you.

Kiss her, caress her face, and her hair but don't head straight for her breasts or her vagina.

Don't forget to brush your teeth and remove bad odour. One of the most off putting things is to have to deal with a spouse whose breath could win a war.

Many women are self conscious about their naked bodies and may want to have intercourse with lights off or with dim lights, which can create a nice atmosphere.

Your woman may not feel comfortable about engaging in sexual intercourse the first night. As the husband, you should be understanding and bear in mind you have your whole life ahead of you to enjoy intimacy.

One quick thrust with the penis will do the job. She may feel very anxious and fearful of the pain she has heard about when having sex for the first time. It may be even easier if she sits on top of the man. That way, she is in control of it all.

If you're a virgin man, finding your wife's vagina for the first time can be tricky.

To make it easier, the woman may want to lie down with her knees bent and her legs spread wide. This will open up the vagina more, making it easier for the husband to penetrate his wife. Use lubricant or olive oil to make it easier to enter into her. The penis will more easily slide in with the application of olive oil.

44

USE LUBRICANT FOR
YOUR WEDDING NIGHT

Couples can face some real challenges when they initially have sex.

Such as:

1. The man cannot achieve a really hard erection, making it hard for him to penetrate his woman every time.

2. The woman is a virgin and despite the hymen being broken, the vagina is extremely tight and still penetrating is hard for the man and painful for her.

3. In attempting to penetrate her, he loses his erection. Sometimes, he can become frustrated by this.

By using natural olive oil, the couple can overcome all the problems above.

The really slippery nature of the oil allows the man's penis to slide in easily. It makes the experience extremely pleasurable for the woman as she will feel the penis slide inside her easily. There will be no friction, so no pain.

Also, a man with a weak erection can penetrate his woman, too.

Once inside, his erection is bound to become much stronger and harder.

It can be used on the woman's breasts, vagina, and other body parts, making the experience more sensual when stroked and caressed.

Make sure you don't use olive oil on a condom as it will damage it.

45

TRY AS MANY
SEX POSITIONS

It's very hard to have an exciting sex life when doing the same positions over and over again. According to some research, the average couple experiments and use one to three positions to have sex. How boooring! Try as many positions as possible. There are virtually hundreds. So, now you both have no excuse to complain of married life being boring. If it is, then it means the romantic or the sex department needs working on. Below are some in no particular order.

46

WOMAN RIDES MAN'S
TONGUE/MOUTH

The man lies on his back on the bed. His woman starts sliding her vagina against his tongue. Apply some olive oil on the vagina and dab some on the tongue. She's in control and can go as fast as she wants.

47

SEX WITH BREASTS/BUTTOCKS

By applying olive oil on the woman's breasts, the man could slide his penis between the woman's breasts. Squeeze her breasts and press them against your penis as you slide up and down them. The man can slide his penis in between her buttocks. This is a great turn on for men.

48

MOVE YOUR PENIS FORWARD UP AND INTO HER

If the man is on top in the classic missionary position, he should move his penis in and out of her at a **diagonal angle**. instead of going straight in and out. This will ensure he rubs her clitoris her place of heaven more. He could also move his entire body in a rhythmic circular motion as opposed to just straight in. You'll notice your woman will move in a circular motion when she gets on top.

49

POWERFUL ORGASMS FOR MEN

Lie down on your back on the bed with your legs flat and apart. Put some olive oil on your penis. Get your woman to gently rub her hands up and down your penis. She should have some olive oil, too. Focus on just the pleasure. Look at the ceiling. Don't be afraid to make grunts of pleasure and other sounds of pleasure. Feel free to make as much noise as you want.

The woman should start slow with feather like touches.

Bear in mind, your man's pleasure points on his penis are: the frenulum, the area located on the under-side of the penis, and the corona.

You, the woman, could use the pad of your thumb and move it in a circular motion against the frenulum. Speed up as your man starts to become more and more excited. Eventually, slide your hand up and down his penis fast. Make sexual moans as you do it.

Increase speed but not her grip. You, the man, should keep looking at the ceiling until you ejaculate. Looking at the ceiling and with your mouth open and eyes slightly closed will give you a powerful orgasm that no words can describe.

Hopefully, you should feel the orgasm in your brain, not just your genitals.

50

YOUR BRAIN IS THE GREATEST CENTRE FOR ORGASMS

This is one of the greatest secrets of sex. If you thought that the greatest place to feel an orgasm is the genitals area alone, you are gravely mistaken. The brain is the place you wanna feel an orgasm, for both the man and woman. Nothing beats it.

So, how do you feel an orgasm and transfer your sexual pleasure from your genitals to your brain?

Easy. Look up to the ceiling, keep your mouth open slightly, and keep your eyes closed slightly. This is the face people make when they are really enjoying sex. Do it and you should feel the pleasure in your brain, which is more powerful than feeling pleasure in your genitals alone. You could use this in any sex position. It really heightens the pleasure. Don't forget, the louder the sounds you make during sex, the more mind-blowing it is likely to be.

51

WOMEN DON'T
CHASE ORGASMS!

A lot of women make the mistake of trying to climax and have an orgasm. Many don't have one. Too many women spend their time during sex 'trying' to have an orgasm. Or chasing an orgasm.

The best way to have an orgasm is to not try and have one. Don't chase it. Let it come to you. Just surrender your body to pleasure and sensation. Enjoy the sex. Focus your attention on enjoying sex. By doing this, you'll not enjoy the experience and if you don't enjoy the sex, you won't have an orgasm.

Same is true for men who find it hard to have an erection. Enjoy the sexual touches of your partner and don't worry about getting an erection; the erection will come. Make the goal of sex to feel good and gain pleasure, NOT HAVE AN ORGASM!

52

THE SURFBOARD POSITION

Get your woman to lie down on her stomach. She could place her chin on her arms or a pillow to sup-port her head. Place a pillow under her stomach. Spread her legs out. Get on top of her. Enter her in a board surfing position. When you thrust, go slowly.

This position can be deeply arousing for men. Going in too fast could cause you to ejaculate too early.

53

A LITTLE CHANGE OF ANGLES CAN MAKE A BIG DIFFERENCE

In the missionary position, the woman could change the angle of her legs. Each slight change in angle, whether opening up her legs and making them wider for deeper penetration, or closing her legs making her vagina tighter, can be the difference between boring, repetitive sex and orgasmic delight! Make as many slight changes in angle as possible by slightly opening and closing your legs. You both should feel the difference. With her legs dangling in the air wide, enter her doing press ups. It's amazing! Hold her by her calves with her legs open wide and you on your knees and slide in and out of her. Bring your woman's legs close together for a different amazing feeling. With the man's arms down, the woman could bring her legs up rest the back of her knees and calves on his arms and he then penetrates her nice and deep. This position will send you both to heaven. The man could go slow or pummel her. Careful you don't hurt her by slipping out of her vagina and hitting the outer part of her vagina. This is very painful. The woman could also rest her feet on her man's buttocks. Now you're gonna wanna have sex every time.

She could place her feet flat on his chest whilst he slides in and out of her for OMG sex. She could place her feet onto his shoulders. She could lay her legs from her buttocks to her toes completely flat, widened or tight. She could wrap her feet around her man. Do the coital alignment technique. He could penetrate her in a circular motion, which will bring both of you a different feeling. Sitting on his knees, he could slide in and out of her whilst putting some of his weight on her breasts and squeezing them. Because missionary is the most common position in sex, varying the different sex positions and techniques in this position is one of the fastest ways to break monotony and boring sex.

Is sex boring now? NO! Couples make it boring. God has made sex extremely pleasurable. It's the couples who aren't trying to make it pleasurable for each other.

Now then, fellow men and women, get in the bedroom and try these suggestions. Forget finishing the rest of this book. Fulfil your carnal desires! Fuck each other's brains out.

54

CONTRACT YOUR PC MUSCLES FOR A TIGHTER EXPERIENCE

Whilst the man is penetrating his woman, the woman could contract her PC muscles. These are the muscles responsible for holding yourself from urinating.

This will make you both feel the experience and feel the full length and diameter of the man's penis sliding and rubbing against the walls of the vagina.

The stronger the woman's PC muscles are, the tighter the grip her vagina will have on her man's penis.

55

THE CLIP POSITION

The woman gets on top of her man but arches her back, supporting herself with her hands on the bed. She could place her hands on his legs for support, too. The angle created by arching her back exposes her clitoris more. The man keeps his legs closed whilst you, the woman, straddle him. This is a great position to achieve orgasm as it makes it easy for her clitoris to rub against his member.

56

JUST BEND OVER

Whilst standing, the woman should bend over and the man should penetrate her. Once inside, the woman should then stand up. Now you can have sex standing up. Here, the man can stimulate your clitoris, grab and squeeze your breasts, kiss your neck, and squeeze your buttocks. So, you, the woman, will receive pleasure in multiple ways. For height differences, the taller spouse should spread their legs more.

57

SPREAD YOUR LEGS

The woman lays in the missionary position, her legs spread wide, bent, with her feet only touching the surface of the bed/floor. The man licks and sucks her vagina gently as well as kissing it with his lips.

58

PRISON GUARD

The woman bends over and her wrists are pulled back and held by the man, who is standing behind and penetrating her. You can adjust your knees for any height differences. The man controls the thrusting. This position allows for deep and forceful penetration.

59

THE 69 POSITION OR MUTUAL ORAL SEX

The woman can get on top of the man, who is lying down. She puts her head above his penis with her butt and vagina hovering above her man's mouth. Both the man and woman lick and mutually give each other oral sex with their tongues. To increase each other's pleasure, you could take it in turns to lick another's genitals so the receiver can focus purely on the pleasure.

60

DOGGY STYLE

The woman can bend over then move onto the edge of the bed. This position allows for deep penetration and clitoral stimulation. The man needs to be careful to not thrust too hard from behind as it can become painful for her. For the man to gain amazing pleasure he should look up to the ceiling, keep his mouth open slightly and his eyes slightly shut. He should feel the orgasms in his brain.

61

REVERSE COWGIRL

The man lies down on his back on the bed. The woman sits on top, facing in the direction of his feet.

Utilising firm grinding motions with her pelvis forward and back, you, the woman, can have a lot of clitoral stimulation, which will help you reach orgasm.

62

THE SLIDE

With the woman on top and with her legs closed, she slides up and down his body. He is lying down just like the previous position.

63

BLOOD RUSH

The man enters his woman in missionary. She moves off the edge of the bed with her head hanging down and he pounds her as hard as he can with his penis. The blood rush to her head, coupled with the penis pounding her, will be ecstasy for her.

64

THE EAGLE

The man sits on his knees in front of his woman, who is lying down. The woman places her legs into the air and spreads them wide apart. He holds her legs apart, varying the speed and thrusts. A great sex position.

65

MISSIONARY SLIGHTLY ALTERED

With you, the woman, on your back, put a pillow under your butt, lift your hips, and pull your legs up and back toward your shoulders, as if you are folded in half. This allows your man to thrust more easily and for deeper penetration.

66

MODIFIED DOGGY STYLE

The woman should lie on her stomach. Lift up her butt so the man can penetrate her. The man could hold himself up in a press up position, or lie on top of her. This is a great way to increase the friction between the man and woman's genitals. With each press up done slowly both should feel the pleasure of both pussy and dick massaging each other.

67

WOMAN AGAINST A WALL BENT OVER

Here, the woman standing could bend over, sup-porting herself with her hands against the wall to sup-port herself. The man enters her, adjusting his knees for height differences. Remember to talk dirty whisper things to her as this will heighten and spice it up.

68

BENT OVER EXOTIC ARAB STYLE

Try this. The woman dresses in erotic sexy Arab hijaab clothing. With the woman standing again, bending over with her legs spread a little, with a straight back, her hands resting on her knees for balance. The man enters, using the woman's torso for support and balance. The man should bring himself as close as possible to the woman, leaning slightly over to add power to his pumping. Role play as if she's a hot erotic Arab chick and the man is touching her sexily, lifting up her clothing, and entering her. She could be Cleopatra and he a handsome ordinary man giving her the pumping her husband can't give her.

69

AN ORGASM PRODUCING POSITION FOR THE WOMAN (I)

She lies on her stomach. The man should enter her with a pillow under her stomach. The man lies fully flat on top of her. The man should move up as high as he can and not try and stay even with her body. The man uses the pillow to position himself and thrusts down. If the man can last eight minutes, then the woman should reach orgasm.

70

ORGASM PRODUCING POSITION FOR THE WOMAN (II)

In the missionary position, place a pillow under her lower back. Once inside her, the man should move her legs onto his shoulders. Here, the man should place his hands between her and the pillow. Now the man should lift her up so he is penetrating his woman in an up and in motion.

71

SEX ON THE STAIRS

The woman kneels over in front of her partner on the staircase. The woman can use the both sides of the banister to support herself, the man holds her hips to support and penetrate her.

72

KEEP YOUR PANTIES ON

"It can be pleasurable torture to play with each other over your underwear, teasing and stroking through the fabric," says sex coach, Patti Britton, Ph.D. "You're building up the anticipation, so when you finally do have skin-on-skin contact, it'll be that much more explosive and exciting."When she lies on her back on the bed with her panties on the man could put his finger into them and start masturbating her vagina. Remember to use olive oil and make movements in a circular way using the middle finger.

73

FIND HER G SPOT

This is one amazing part of a woman's body for pleasure.

If stimulated, it can give quicker and more intense orgasms.

To find the G-spot, insert the forefinger into the vagina and rest the finger tip on the front wall, about two thirds of the way along the vagina toward the cervix.

You should feel a small configuration of muscles that are able to resist firm but gentle pressure.

Don't forget, as a man, you can give her an orgasm through her vagina, G spot and clitoral orgasm.

74

STIMULATE YOUR WOMAN'S CLITORIS

Master the art of stimulating your woman's clitoris. Many men don't realize this is important and believe an effective way of pleasuring the woman is to go in and out with their penis a dozen times. Did you know a few gentle rubs against your woman's clitoris will send her into a wild mode? So you don't need to work hard to get her to have an orgasm if you stimulate this part of her anatomy. When men masturbate it is the frenulum part that they rub to bring themselves to orgasm and ejaculate. Women masturbate by rubbing their clitoris. If you can stimulate her clitoris you won't need to last longer. Want proof? See how long she lasts when she gets on top and grinds you the man. No very long right? Why because her clit is being stimulated.

The woman's clitoris can be stimulated in the following ways:

- By placing a pillow under her lower back in the missionary position.

- In missionary position, get her to lay her legs flat and narrow.

- In the missionary position, instead of your legs inside hers, place them outside hers. Her legs together or narrowed will cause the head of your penis to rub your woman's clitoris.

- In the missionary position, thrust into your woman in a circular motion as if you're stirring a drink with your penis.

- Coital alignment (discussed earlier)

- In the missionary position, place a pillow under her butt. Apply lubricant. Place your penis flat against her vulva with the head aimed at the clitoris. Stroke back and forth as if you were inside your woman's vagina. Each stroke will cause the penis to rub against the vulva and the head will hit the clitoris, causing her to go into an orgasmic mode. The penis stays outside the vagina the whole time.

- Use the pad of your middle finger to stimulate in circles or up and down.

- Oral sex. Gently kissing, licking, and sucking with the lips and tongue.

75

FOUR STEPS TO GIVE THE WOMAN A SCREAMING ORGASM THROUGH INTERCOURSE ALONE

1. Make her feel like she is the sexiest woman alive and let her know how much she turns you on. During foreplay, worship her erogenous zones.

2. Give extreme clitoral stimulation, oral or other-wise, as early as possible.

3. Encourage her to scream as loudly as possible and not be afraid of expressing her pleasure.

4. Stamina. Have your woman masturbate your penis daily, using the edging technique. Desensitizing yourself to her touches will build your ability to last longer in bed. It'll give you harder erections that are likely to cause her to orgasm faster, too. Remember it's not about just how big but very importantly how HARD you are that'll pleasure your woman.

76

HOW TO TURN ON
YOUR WOMAN

Women are "secretly horny." So why is she not grabbing her man and wanting to have sex with him regularly? For the woman to act on her secret sexual desires she needs a few things.

1. The man needs to "wake up" her sexual desires by drawing her attention to them in ways she will be responsive.

2. The man needs to reassure the woman to act on her sexual desires freely without the fear of him judging her to be slutty. Encourage her.

3. He needs to make her feel incredibly sexy and get over her insecurities about her body and go after him.

So, how do you all of that?

Remember, men are visual creatures. Men get turned on by what they see. A lot of men are addicted to porn and find it hard to stop.

Men get sexually excited by what they see. That's why women taking off their clothes and appearing naked in front of their men, will turn them on in a second. Women are turned on by what they **feel** and **imagine**. The fact of the matter is, women's biggest erogenous zone is their minds.

That's why just giving her gifts and taking her out to dinner will make her love you more and make her grateful but it may NOT always turn her on. The way you get your woman to throw you down on the bed for steamy sex is through **sexy stories**,(with yourselves as the characters of course) **sexy situations** role playing for example, and **sexy language**. Here's proof. Why do you think many women like to read romantic novels? Why do you think the majority of readers of 50 shades of grey are women? The language used in these novels turns women on.

"She cried out, for he was there between her legs, and it was his tongue now touching her, tasting her, laving up her essence. – **Splendor**

Notice as mentioned previously, the focus is on what the man is doing TO the woman and not the other way around. She is the receiver of sexual pleasure.

Her pelvis was pressed hard against his, gyrating pulling him even more deeply into the velvet warm walls of her femininity. – **Wild Abandon**

Believe it or not most romance novels contain this sort of language. Even more graphic language.

Can you see? A combination of the **story**, **situation** and **sexy language** is what turns women on.

If the woman sends a sexy picture of herself to the man, wears no clothes in front of him that will turn him on.

For the woman **language** and **imagery** are the things that will turn her on.

Pick any story and you'll find "innocent" women who are suddenly unable to control themselves and cannot control their lust.

Romance novels are packed full of language specifically designed to reach the pleasure part of her mind that turns her on.

So, how does the man deliver these things that will turn on the woman? Simple. Through text messages. Use the steamy material exactly as it is from romance books but change the pronouns from he to **I** (meaning you the man) and her to **you** meaning the woman.

'**You** cried out, for **I** was there between **your** legs, and it was my tongue now touching **you**, tasting **you**, laving up **your** essence.

Send the messages during the day. With sex text messages you can have secret dirty sexual fantasy based conversations with your woman. This will wake up her sexual desires. You'll be feeding your woman with sexual fantasies with yourself that she is designed to respond to sexually. Also, we know as humans we are more likely to say things in text than we are verbally. People say things and open up more through text messages. They are more likely to say more of what is on their minds. Imagine how much you'll both open up to each other via text messages. Things that may have been hard to say verbally become so much easier via text.

Below is an example that had me so horny I got wet and grabbed my husband in through the door as soon as he opened it. He wrote the text from outside our house front door. I did nothing except spread my legs and receive his warm hard dick. "Screw foreplay just get inside me" I said.

You led the way to the front door and locked it. The front door closed and I jerked you into my arms. The kiss was hot, hungry, passionate.

You found yourself melting into it, sinking into my touch, seduced and how I so expertly commanded you with one touch. You pushed at my shoulders. "I'm sup-posed to be mad at you."

"Be mad at me later. Fuck me now." I didn't let you reply, i just swept you off your feet and carried you across our open plan house

We made it to the dining table. I kicked the chairs away and set you on the edge. Though we'd had sex on most of the furniture, this was new. You clawed at my trouser zip yanking it down. The Fabric ripped.

Your legs hung off the side and your heels dropped to the floor, discarded

Cool air skates over your breasts. You'd weren't wearing a bra since you knew I liked that, so there was nothing to shield your breasts when I pulled your clothes off you animalistic with no boundaries.

My narrowed gaze devoured your body, touching you with dark intent.

I pushed you down onto the table and held you there with one hand on your stomach and stripped your panties off you.

I stepped between your knees, pushing them open.

Your heart still beating little harder the first moment I saw you completely exposed. You are my feast, spread out for the taking.

I didn't waste time touching or caressing, but we often didn't have time for that. I cupped your ass in both hands; you flattened your hands against the table and held your breath as I licked the length of your clit.

I sucked on your clit, I surprised you when I suddenly penetrated you. Just thinking about what we were doing and where was so hot.

I pulled you to the edge of the table and thrust into you. You gasped and gripped the edge, as your vagina wettened and stretched to accommodate my warm hard dick. The feel of my dick inside you was growing more familiar. I leaned over you, forcing you back almost to your elbows and thrusting, sinking fully into you.

I bend my head and suck one nipple. You push your fingers through my hair and squeeze my dick, gripping it tightly with your vaginal muscles. It feels as if there was a thread of sensation tied from your breast to your pussy,. At long last I begin to thrust, in and out of your pussy. The sound of breathing, of our joining bodies, you groan and moan as You take with your left hand the base of my dick and start vibrating my dick inside you.

You grow hornier and hornier FUCK ME YOU BASTARD! you demand

I start drilling you mercilessly with my wet hard rod. The familiar sound of our juices joining mixing and making squelching sounds begins as I continue to pummel your horny wet warm pussy.

Oh Steve give it to me ! You shriek

Your orgasm rolls up through your body, warm and all-consuming, you shudder and whimper as I continue to fuck you violently. Your juice starts dripping out of your pussy uncontrollably

Sparks of sensation coursed through Your veins, drawing the orgasm out longer as I hit the perfect spot within you. You almost cry out, the pleasure becoming too much, but I thrust deep and groaned.

The pounding of your pussy continues and you say

Oh Steve give me your juice cum inside me ! You want me to cum?

Yes

Oh Sarah!

I'm gonna explode inside YOU!

Suddenly you feel my warm thick, wet cum shoot inside you. It feels amazing.

You pant relieved I'd cum. My dick now slowly massages the walls of your vagina as the night of passion draws to a close.

I pull my dick out.

Wipe your cum drenched vagina then my dick and lie next to you.

Oh Steve I want another vagina massage. You're so dirty.

In short women get turned on by how a man touches them or by words he uses. Many men complain about the lack of sex. But don't realize it's up to them to get their women turned up. You have to give get her wet in order to sink your dick into her.

77

SEXTING EACHOTHER

Send really sexy, explicit messages to each other's phones. Images should be avoided as this could fall into the wrong hands. The man could be on your way home from work when he sends it. The woman could send one to her man.

Examples of sexting:

- When will you b home in bd w/ me?

- Get off early from work and come get me.

- I wanna taste your cum.

- Get home so I can bang you all night long.

- What you wearing right now?

- I wana sink my big wet warm hard cock inside you!

- Come and spread my legs

- Open me up wide for your dick

- I wanna slide down your penis

- My penis/vagina is dripping wet.

- I want to ride your penis

- I wanna make you wet w/ my juice

- On the bed w/o clothes pussy dripping with cum

- My penis/vagina is so hot!

- I'm gonna suck your pussy dry

- I'm gonna ram/pummel/pound you

- Squirt all over me

- I'm gonna scream your name

- My legs are spread and ready.

- I wana drill you with my cock.

- The head of my penis is warm bulging and wants to feel the warm walls of your vagina.

- I wana stand behind you run my hands up your legs up your skirt onto your chest and squeeze your breasts and fuck you until your cum starts running down your legs.

- I wana stand behind you, with my hard erect cock pressed against your sexy buttocks and run my fingers up your inner thighs and play with your pussy.

- I'm gonna bang you so hard that your breasts will make slapping sounds.

- My pussy's wet waiting for your dick to fill it up.

- You're gonna love the feeling of my wet hard warm cock sliding in and of you.

- Explode your cum inside me NOW!

- RAM ME HARD!

- FUCK MY BRAINS OUT!

- Once inside you, you won't want me out.

- I'm gonna pound you until you pass out.

78

ENJOY A RAUNCHIE QUICKIE

You're both on your way out to meet friends, or going for dinner to your family's house. But she just looks so sexy and alluring in that dress. He looks sexy, too. Pin her against a wall. Kiss her hard. Kiss her neck from behind. Feel her up (her clothes on) from her legs to her vagina, and squeeze her breasts. Pin her to the bed and rock her world for ten minutes. Pummel her like an animal. Fulfil both your carnal desires. Having sex quickly is amazing! It'll bring the animal out of you. And the horny whore out of her.

79

BEST TIMES WOMEN
HAVE BETTER ORGASMS

Women have the best orgasms between 1PM and 5PM. It's true, they do. A perfect reason to have sex and then go to sleep for an afternoon siesta. Working? Do it on a weekend or your days off. Go home for lunch.

80

BE SPONTANEOUS

DON'T, DON'T, DON'T schedule sex. Don't agree on a time and place you're gonna have sex with your spouse. That is sooooo boring. It needs to be un-planned and spontaneous. There is nothing wrong with the man planning his sexual moves in advance for future sex sessions but knowing when and where you're gonna have sex is a major turn off.

81

DON'T JUST HAVE SEX! MAKE LOVE

Is there a difference between making love and having sex? If you've experienced both, then you'll know the difference. Sex by itself is an animalistic act. Nothing wrong with it, as we are all horny, no matter what our beliefs. Making love, however, means during sex, you are emotionally connected to your spouse. It maybe because of one doing a very kind act for the other. When the man penetrates, both can become emotional during sex. It's no longer a case of the penis just entering in and out the vagina. It's now a time for the couple to bond. Having sex is for pleasure. Making love, which can provide more pleasure, involves a deep bonding and connection felt between both during intercourse.

82

HOW TO RE-IGNITE THE SEX IN YOUR RELATIONSHIP

You've just had a baby weeks go by before you have sex. You're tired exhausted your man complains that it's months since you last had sex.

So how do you bring the sex back into your relationship post baby delivery?

1. Branch Out

You're afraid of waking the baby during sex so the bedroom is a no no. So what do you do? Why not have sex in the living room? Get a water bed and use that instead.

Use the sofa. It's fun different and exciting from the normal routine of your bedroom.

2. Maximise naptime

During weekdays use naptime to do house work or catch up on sleep. But when your man is off why not use it to catch up on some sex on a mid afternoon Sunday?

3. Talk about the old days

Have a meal as a couple and talk about the old days before you became parents. Talk about all the fun times, the holidays the dinners out and anything else you can think that was fun romantic enjoyable you'll find yourselves in the mood for sex.

4. Alone time

Drop the baby off to one of your parent's house hire a baby sitter once a week. DO whatever and once you're out alone BAN all baby talk. Act how you used to act when you first met each other. It's MAGIC! Pretty soon you'll be in bed having great sex.

5. Don't wait for the perfect time

Never wait for the perfect time. The time will never be just right. Don't wait for privacy babies have no idea what's happening so just get to business. If you have a Moses basket just move it into another part of the house if you're still not comfortable.

6. Sext Away

Whilst at work the guy could sext his Mrs describing in graphic detail what he wants to do to her when he gets home. This will set the mood. He could even do it when he is just five minutes away from the house. So if he is really good at Sexting she'll grab him into bed at the door. Tip: Make sure oh men you have a shower at work if you can or at least have fresh breath before you reach home buy some fresh mint gum.

7. Showers

Whilst the baby is asleep. The woman should have a shower that's a sure way to feel horny. Even better if you both have a shower together but minimally the woman should have a shower to get "in the mood."

83

MISSIONARY VARIATIONS

It can get rather boring when you do the same position again and again. Below are some variations.

- Woman lies on her back from her bed up to her bum with her legs dangling off the edge. This gives deeper great penetration.

- She wraps her legs around his bum.

- She wraps her legs around his back.

- Places pillow under her bum or back.

- Coital alignment

- Woman lies on back places her feet on his chest.

- Lifts her legs in air bringing them together.

- She places her feet on his shoulders.

- As he enters in any of above variations she con-tracts her PC muscles.

- She sits up and sits on his thighs

- He sits on his knees holds her by her sides and enters her in a forward fashion.

84

SEX TOOLS

Wedge ramp

Allows you to enjoy sex in a non flat position great for enhancing and making missionary sex last longer.

You'll definitely enjoy many different positions with these new mattresses sold on Amazon.

Durex Little devil vibrating ring

Feeling a little lazy to give your woman great foreplay? Wana skip the intro and get straight to the action? Introducing Durex's vibrating ring.

Although designed to be placed on the penis. The man won't get much pleasure placing this on his penis. It's great when the woman lies down in the missionary position and the man puts it around his middle and index finger wearing it like a ring. It's easier for him to control the ring brushing the woman's clit going gently up and down.

Within a minute of using this ring she'll be fired up as it gives amazing clitoral stimulation. The woman can direct her man telling him how and where she wants him to use it.

You2toys intimate spreader

- Finds G spot
- Spreads the labia for amazing deeper penetration
- Stronger orgasms
- Gives her an amazing view of his semen inside. Available On Amazon.

Twister

A great tool for pre sex. You can play with clothes on. Each time you lose you take an item of clothing off. Or you can play this naked from the start. The thrill of your naked bodies touching each other can be real hot. Why not make it a challenge that the man has to try and penetrate his woman in the different positions they find themselves in.

BONUS SECTIONS TEASE HER

Women enjoy talking when they don't have to get straight to the point. They like to circle around giving themselves time to discover gradually what they want to say. This is exactly how women enjoy sex. Women love men who take their time to get to the point.

For example instead of touching her breasts directly, a man should circle them getting closer and closer. When he gets close enough he could move somewhere else and start anew.

He could slowly move up her inner thighs and just when his fingers or lips are close to her vagina and she expects him to touch her there he could move over to the other side. He could kiss her around her pubic bone area her stomach his lips closely hovering over her vagina. Repeating this process will build her excitement.

SHE NEEDS TO RELAX

Men want to have orgasms so they can relax. But unlike men, women must relax first before she can enjoy great sex and orgasm.

Through great teasing and foreplay a woman can relax and let go to enjoy sex.

One thing she can do to relax before sex is have a long hot bath. Once done she's more likely going to be in the mood to enjoy sex. She'll be more sensitive to his feather like touches.

Relaxation and gentle foreplay are the foundations for awakening a woman's arousal. Play some sexual erotic music in the background when you start foreplay. This will really help her relax even faster.

A SLOW HAND

As a woman, when my husband caresses me with his slow hand I can feel my arousal build up gradually. I can feel the fire of desire slowly getting hotter and hotter. By touching my non erogenous zones slowly with his hand by the time he gets to my inner thighs I'm already wet. To get an idea of what a slow hand means watch erotic sex scene movies and see how slow the man moves with his hand when he caresses a woman. Notice his slow feather like gentle touches. Touching her slowly will bring her to climax quicker during intercourse. Never enter a woman unless she is at least wet.

HOW TO MAKE HER REEALLY WET

A man should take two fingers the index and middle.

He should place them on the left and right side of her vagina (Labia Majora) forming a v shape with them. Then, massage the left and right side of her vagina (Labia Majora) in an up and down motion. Many people do not know a woman's clitoris is not just on the outside but also some of it extends along the left and right sides of her vagina.

By massaging this area this will get her soaking wet and maybe even orgasm. Get a stopwatch so you can time yourself doing this for a three to five minutes.

HOW TO GET YOUR WOMAN HORNY

A lot of men complain "my wife or girlfriend does not wana have sex." Men need to learn to turn their women on.

Below are eleven great ways they can do this

Sexting describe what you will do to her vagina how hard, slow, deep fast you'll drill your cock into her. Using words like ram, pound drill. Send her erotica sex scenes with you and her as the characters in it.

Hot baths Get Her to take a long HOT bath this will relax her easily, awaken her sexual energy and make her more easily aroused to sex. She could even hint saying she wants sex by stating she is gonna have a long hot bath.

Read Get Her reading sex scenes of romance novels and erotica stories. Put a book mark on them. Or stick her favorite scene on the wall above the headboard so she reads it just before she goes bed. Leave diagrams of her favorite sex positions above the headboard.

Kiss her long romantically gently slowly without touching her anywhere sexually. The longer she enjoys the kiss and melts into it the more aroused she will become. Her mouth has glands which create sexual energy. Sex for a women begins with a kiss creating sexual energy which moves to her breasts then down to her vagina.

Sensual massage involves gentle massaging of the vagina, labia majora, clitoris and buttocks area inserting two fingers into her vagina whilst she relaxes lying down on her stomach on her back with her legs spread.

Smelling great always when you get back from work wear good perfume and check your breath. Smelling great looking great makes women think yum yum. Wear uniform like police, army women love men in uniforms.

Suck lick her nipples gently she should feel excited down below. To get her fired up wild Lick/suck her nipples then start stroking her clitoris at the same time.

Change of environment/bed this allows her to be free from being responsible for the family the house her job. The more beautiful the environment the more relaxed she becomes. The more relaxed she becomes the more in the mood she becomes for sex. Rent a beautiful hotel room by the hour.

Romance read my chapter on touch her heart and she'll let you touch her vagina.

Talk dirty in her ear in a slow smooth deep voice.

Watch how effortlessly Pierce Brosnan in James Bond moves talks looks at women with his eyes. Watch how he speaks. Slow down when you speak and talk smoothly, pause in between words whilst looking into her eyes.

Environment Start making the home environment more sexual. Sexual romantic red color bed sheets, sex toys, hot sexual scenes written and placed above headboard of the bed, erotica novels, sex guides placed near on bedside cabinet, orgasm enhancing gel, sex position diagrams in above bed that she likes, sex sofa, sex door swing, clitoral vibrator, scented bedroom. The more sex is around her the more she is likely to think about it If your home environment has sex toys, erotica novels, sex furniture what is more likely to be on her mind? Sex right? The world has become hooked to sex becomes it's all around us. How sexualized is your home?

Sometimes Steve will sit with his head rested against the headboard of the bed. He'll talk about why he loves me and how he finds each part of my body sexy and beautiful. At the same time he will kiss me on my shoulder blades, neck, earlobes and then with his finger place one of my nipples between his thumb and index finger and start rubbing it gently. Next thing I ask to kiss my nipples and before you know it I want his dick. Sometimes we'll sit naked and talk it's very romantic especially when he talks about why he loves me.

So there you have it guys eleven gates that lead to her vagina.

DON'T FORGET HER PENIS

Did you know that 98% of the orgasms women experience is a result of the stimulation of the clitoris?

Not touching the clitoris is like a woman not stimulating a man's penis. The clitoris is the woman's penis. It is made up the same muscle the penis is made of and becomes erect just like a penis. If you don't believe me, just type on Google images erect clitoris and clitoris diagram. You'll see the clitoris looks like a penis. Because it is an actual penis. And when it's excited it gets erect.

Having spoken to many women, one of the biggest complaints they raise is their man does not touch their clitoris. Either he does not touch her clitoris correctly to arouse her or he does not touch her there long enough. Men may think they have touched her clitoris for a long time but if they actually time themselves they will find that they have only touched her there for a minute or just over a minute. The next time the man strokes her clitoris he should have a stop clock on hand time himself and stroke her that for no less than five minutes or until she is satisfied.

HOW TO MASTURBATE
HER CLITORIS

Using two fingers with the clitoris hood down make circles in a very gentle feather like fashion.

Make sure your fingers are lubricated so the friction does not hurt her.

You could do small circles then big circles. You could go clockwise or anti clockwise. Press down a little BUT not hard.

You can use different fingers. You can even go in an up and down motion. To add to her excitement go fast then slow then fast again then slow. If your fingers get tired use your tongue. Flicking your tongue over her clitoris will really get her juices pouring out.

LET HER PLAY WITH HERSELF

Sometimes when me and Steve are in bed. I may become horny. I know Steve maybe too tired to give me foreplay. So I masturbate myself to a point where all Steve has to do is insert his penis inside me and I reach my climax. This is amazing coz Steve does not need to worry about lasting in order for me to climax. All he has to do is roll over and get inside me. Sometimes Steve's just come from work and I'm masturbating myself he joins in knowing he can focus solely on his pleasure and I can focus on mine.

RECOGNIZE HER SEXUAL MOODS

One of the benefits of letting the man lead is she can think less and feel more and enjoy more. The freedom to relax and not worry about what to do next allows the woman to focus her mind on her own sexual pleasure.

Some days she may feel like an innocent virgin girl experiencing her man's touch for the first time. Here I like to roleplay with my husband. He acts as a priest and I the innocent young virgin nun. I wear a nun's clothing to make it feel more real.

We say things like

"Oh father I don't think you should be touching me like this." As he lifts my dress exposing my naked legs caressing them.

"Oh father stop, this is sinful." As he starts kissing my neck from behind and squeezing my covered breasts I feel his hard erect dick pressing against my buttocks.

"Would you like my holy rod (penis) to pierce and bless your sinful hole?"

"Oh yes father"

As he enters and bangs me hard and fast I exclaim from Ecstasy. "OH YES FATHER BLESS ME BLESS ME with your Holy water."

One role play me and Steve love to play is I am a young virgin nun. And in order to be accepted by the priest. I have to prove my piety by resisting wanting to have sex. Steve acting as a priest will do anything to me to try and get me aroused. From kissing me whilst rubbing my clit. Sucking my breasts, bending down on his knees licking and sucking my clit. Rubbing the head of his penis against my clit. Or whilst I'm standing I have to rub my clit against his hanging tongue and fuck it. If I resist his dick I pass if I don't and have sex with him I fail.

Other days a woman will feel assertive and tell him to lie down and do what she wants with him. Other days she might feel like a snake wanting to wrap her body around his.

CONTROL THYSELF

If a man gets too excited too fast then he will lose control and ejaculate too early. It is absolutely essential that a man maintains control of his emotions early on during sex from foreplay to intercourse by keeping his mind calm. Why's that you ask?

Well when a man feels passion and maintains control, the woman can relax let go of control and start to enjoy her passions. She becomes more relaxed and focused on her pleasure. The more he controls his passions the more she loses control over hers. Maintaining control allows her to achieve increased pleasure whilst in turn allowing him to enjoy more intense orgasms when he ejaculates.

CHANGE PENETRATION PACE

I have something to admit here. Sometimes when me and Steve used to have sex. He'd be on top and then all of a sudden. His primary move on top was getting boring for the both of us. And the passion just dies. It happened twice and well to be honest sometimes sex is not going to be explosive as you expected and that's ok. As long as the couple are willing to practice getting better then it's fine.

Just when we were enjoying sex over a year ago Steve and I both noticed the same type of penetration was just not working.

That's when he started to change it up. Suddenly, Steve started to penetrate fast in my pussy shallow just allowing the head of his penis to enter in and out. That got my juices going a lot and my pulse racing. Then he decided to slow down and penetrate me shallow, then fast and deep, then slow and deep, then hard and deep. OMG IT WAS AMAZING It was so unpredictable, so exciting. Just when I thought things could not get any better he started to vibrate his hip which caused his cock to vibrate inside me. He vibrated his hip sideways left to right rapidly super fast that kept his dick inside me and vibrating. Then he went super sonic ultra fast by vibrating his hip forwards and back so his cock head stayed in but his whole cock would VIBRATE in and out of my vagina. This made me start scratching him until I orgasm and told him "I'm done Steve take your pleasure."

He does this vibration of his hips in missionary and when I go on top of him.

And that's the beauty people. A man by changing the speed of his penetration can bring huge orgasmic pleasure to his woman.

So what are the penetration speeds and types?

-Hard

-Gentle

-Rhythmic (In between fast and slow penetration)

-Slow

-Fast

- Deep

-Shallow

-Vibrating hip vibrating cock (cock needs remain inside for her to feel this)

A little variation in the depth and speed of penetration makes a world of difference

7 MORE SEX TIPS

There's a few more sex tips that me and Steve have done a few times that I wana share with you. Remember, don't feel this is too much info to take in and try. Each time you have sex just remember to try two or three max that Make Her Squirt contains.

1. Whilst giving her oral instead of just going up and down with your tongue which can get boring write the letters of the alphabet with it. Draw a figure 8 or other numbers.

2. One reason women can't relax during sex is because of self image. Keep lights low use a dim light.

3. Spread Nutella chocolate over her body breasts and nipples lick/suck it off slowly.

4. The slower he goes the longer he will last.

5. Sucking a woman's nipples whilst stroking her clitoris at the same time can make her very HORNY!

6. A skilled lover knows to touch a woman's LEAST erogenous zones FIRST such as her back, hair, hands.

7. Women need foreplay to relax and build up their excitement, only enter a woman once she's wet

LAZY FOREPLAY

Sometimes Steve can be too tired for foreplay. So he gets out the Durex vibrator ring. Places the ring his middle and index finger dabbing some olive oil and runs it slowly up and down my clitoris.

It gets really amazing when I get on top grind his cock and at same time starts using the vibrator on my clitoris.

85

SEX SESSION CHECKLIST

Tick off the checklist below to experience amazing steamy sex during each session. See which ones you're doing as a couple and which ones you're not.

- Turn your woman on, through sexy stories, sexy situations and sexy language. Make her imagine a great hot sex scene with you. Touch her kiss her in a sexually arousing manner.

- Role play.

- Foreplay caressing kissing.

- Dirty talk using questions and a foreign language.

- Have sex in different places at home or change the venue.

- Try different positions.

- Make yourselves smell and look good for each other.

- Dress up for each other sexily. Be as sexily pro-vocative as possible.

- Behaving like animals for raunchy sex.

- Woman acting slutty.

- Give her pleasure in more places than one.

- Oral sex. Woman's vagina riding man's mouth and tongue.

- Fingering of woman's vagina.

- Woman on top positions.

- Woman being loud with her voice as opposed to suppressing it. (sure way to reach orgasm)

- Before sex have a warm shower together and after, too!

- Apply oil to the woman's body, breasts, chest, etc., and massage her all over.

- Make sure you touch her clitoris with your penis during sex. Grind her the way she grinds you whilst on top!

- Always use lubricant.

- Women should change the angle and position of their legs.

- Pummel and pound her vagina.

- See each other having sex in the mirror.

- Record a sex video of yourselves having sex. Using a phone mount. Watch it together afterward.

- Have sexual webcam sessions

- Don't forget, different sex techniques make women climax faster.

- Women can take control of their sexual pleasure whilst in missionary position by moving their legs into different angles and positions.

- Enjoy a raunchy quickie.

- Sext each other and send sex voice messages to each other.

- Have phone sex.

- Have dry sex (dry humping).

- Give her vaginal, clitoral, or G-spot orgasms.

- Give him a great hand job with him lying on the bed using olive oil.

- Flirt and seduce each other.

- During sex, turn off your phones and stop all distractions.

- Romantic music playing in the background during a sex session.

- Play sex games. Download a few sex games apps and play them together.

- Women should wear socks. Keeping their feet warm during sex will help them climax faster.

- During each sex session try at least two to three sex positions. This'll keep things fresh.

- Have sex on the bed, sometimes under the duvet or sometimes totally naked and exposed.

- Have sex with her top on and her skirt down.

- Get the woman to sit on your lap with her top on, buttocks exposed, and giving you oral sex

- Pregnant women orgasm very quickly so it's a golden chance to have sex and make her climax.

- Stimulate both sides of her labia Majora to get her really wet

- Stimulate her clitoris in circular motions

- Stimulate her clitoris and suck her nipples at the same time.

- The man should control his passions so she can open up and lose control of herself.

- Use a stopwatch to time foreplay and clitoral stimulation.

- Use sexting, hot baths, and other things to arouse her.

- Relax breathe deep and slow and relax your mind to last longer.

- Make sex goals for various locations and countries you've had and wana have sex. E.g at back of a limo, in a park after closing time, in an open field in a sleeping bag in a Shanghai hotel, in a Turkish water park.

- Hang diagrams above your headboard to remind you of different sex positions to try so you don't forget before sex.

- In missionary let your penis go in and out of her at a diagonal angle as this will make it easier to rub her clitoris more easily.

- Bring her to close to climax and then stop let her energy settle then again bring her close again stop do this three times and then give her an orgasm when she finally orgasms it will be explosive.

- Stimulate her clitoris, vagina, breasts, nipples, in a circular manner. God created women's bodies circular to remind us to stimulate their bodies in a circular manner.

CONCLUSION

There you have it. The guide to HOT STEAMY SEX.

Oh, just one quick story. A beautiful woman called Alisha, once married. On their wedding night, her husband made love to her no fewer than seven times, so that when morning came, she told him, "You are a perfect in every way, even in this!" So men, as you are the giver of pleasure, the onus is upon you to educate yourselves on pleasuring your women. The question on every woman's mind is how hard, how often and how much?

MAKE HER SQUIRT truly is the key to enjoying a great sex life.

When sex becomes a chore for your woman, it means your relationship is in serious danger of becoming dead. Save it by applying the sexual practices and techniques mentioned in this book.

Apply these techniques to your sex life. And you will have such amazing, OMG sex that you'll both wanna tell a close friend!

Now get in that bedroom and give your woman the greatest sexual pleasure she has ever had in her life! Bang her like a champ her vagina wants it!

SIGNS OF PLEASURE

So how do you know if you're woman is enjoying sex?

Here is a list of signs.

- She passes out from extreme pleasure.

- Ejaculates her own cum.

- She's scratching her man's back whilst enjoying great sex in the missionary position.

- Her mouth becomes dry

- She conks out after a few minutes

- She madly pulls you demanding you to get back inside her

- She waits for you asking if you're coming to bed.

- Whilst on top of her man she collapses to the bed.

- She becomes drained of energy after sex finishes.

- Wants her man to hold her in his arms. After each session the man should go through this list then he'll have a good idea if the woman is enjoying sex.

Thank you for reading Make Her Squirt I hope you've found the tips helpful. If so, please leave a review for it on Amazon, and recommend it to a friend I am so grateful that you have taken the time to find ways to enjoy sex more.

ABOUT THE AUTHOR

Sarah Johansson is a happily married mother of two. She's been married for five years. She resides in New York with her husband. She works as a sex therapist, helping women to discuss and solve their relationship and sexual problems.

CPSIA information can be obtained
at www.ICGtesting.com
Printed in the USA
BVOW06s0245080617
486378BV00007B/45/P

9 781534 892149